Abbey Road : The Beatles

WISE PUBLICATIONS
London/New York/Sydney/Paris

Exclusive Distributors:
MUSIC SALES LIMITED
8/9 Frith Street,
London W1V 5TZ, England.
MUSIC SALES PTY LIMITED
120 Rothschild Avenue,
Rosebery, NSW 2018,
Australia.

This book © Copyright 1992 by Wise Publications
Order No.NO90537
ISBN 0-7119-3261-1

Music arranged by Frank Booth
Music processed by MSS Studios
Book design by Pearce Marchbank Studio
Computer origination by Adam Hay

Music Sales' complete catalogue lists thousands of titles
and is free from your local music shop, or direct from
Music Sales Limited. Please send a cheque/postal order
for £1.50 for postage to: Music Sales Limited,
Newmarket Road, Bury St. Edmunds, Suffolk IP33 3YB.

YOUR GUARANTEE OF QUALITY
As publishers, we strive to produce every book to the
highest commercial standards.
The music has been freshly engraved and the book has
been carefully designed to minimise awkward page turns
and to make playing from it a real pleasure.
Particular care has been given to specifying acid-free,
neutral-sized paper which has not been chlorine bleached
but produced with special regard for the environment.
Throughout, the printing and binding have been planned
to ensure a sturdy, attractive publication which should
give years of enjoyment.
If your copy fails to meet our high standards,
please inform us and we will gladly replace it.

Printed in the United Kingdom by
Halstan & Co Limited, Amersham, Buckinghamshire.

COME TOGETHER

Words & Music by John Lennon & Paul McCartney.

**Moderately slow,
with double tempo feel**

1. Here come old flat-top, He come groov-ing up slow-ly, He got

Joo Joo eye-ball, He one ho-ly roll-er, He got hair down

to his knee. __ Got to be a jok-er, He just do what he please. __

2. He wear no shoe-shine, He got toe - jam foot-ball, He got
3. He bag pro-duc-tion, He got wal - rus gum-boot, He got
4. He rol - ler-coast-er, He got ear - ly warn-ing, He got

mon - key fin-ger, He shoot Co-ca Co-la; He say, "I know __ you
O - no side-board, He one spi-nal crack-er, He got feet down be-low __
mud - dy wa-ter, He one mo-jo fil-ter, He say "One and one and one __

SOMETHING

Words & Music by George Harrison.
© Copyright 1969 Harrisongs Limited.
All Rights Reserved. International Copyright Secured.

MAXWELL'S SILVER HAMMER

Words & Music by John Lennon & Paul McCartney.
© Copyright 1969 Northern Songs, under licence to
MCA Music Limited, 77 Fulham Palace Road, London W6.
All Rights Reserved. International Copyright Secured.

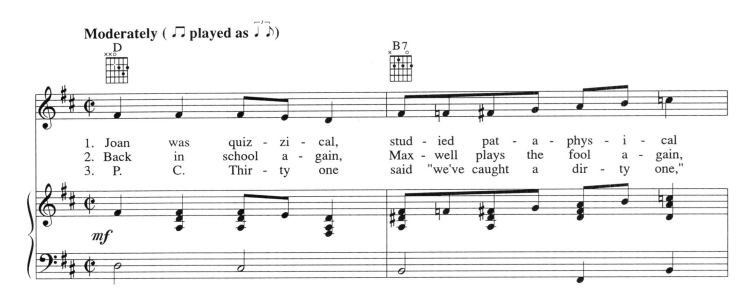

1. Joan was quiz-zi-cal, stud-ied pat-a-phys-i-cal
2. Back in school a-gain, Max-well plays the fool a-gain,
3. P. C. Thir-ty one said "we've caught a dir-ty one,"

sci-ence in the home. ____ Late nights all a-lone ____
Teach-er gets an-noyed. ____ Wish-ing to a-void
Max-well stands a-lone. ____ Paint-ing tes-ti-mo-

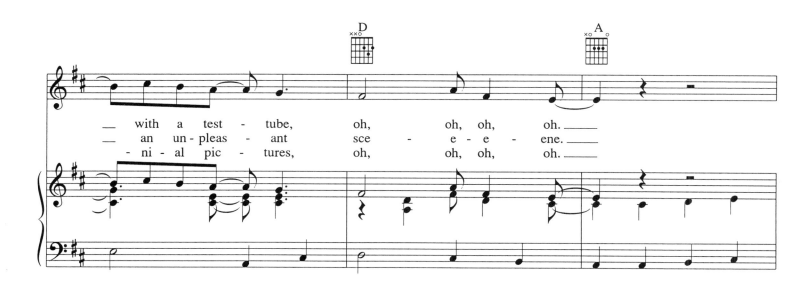

____ with a test-tube, oh, oh, oh, oh. ____
____ an un-pleas-ant sce-e-ene. ____
-ni-al pic-tures, oh, oh, oh, oh. ____

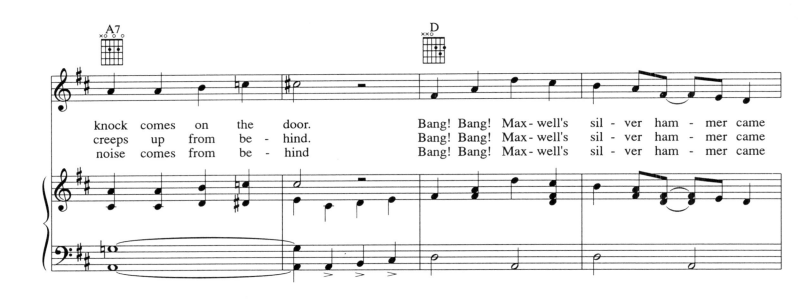

knock comes on the door.
creeps up from be - hind.
noise comes from be - hind

Bang! Bang! Max - well's sil - ver ham - mer came
Bang! Bang! Max - well's sil - ver ham - mer came
Bang! Bang! Max - well's sil - ver ham - mer came

down up - on her head. ___
down up - on her head. ___
down up - on his head. ___

Clang! Clang! Max - well's sil - ver ham - mer made

sure that she was dead. ___

sure that she was dead. ___

To Coda ⊕   D.C. al Coda

⊕ Coda

Sil - ver ham - mer.

OH! DARLING

Words & Music by John Lennon & Paul McCartney.

OCTOPUS'S GARDEN

Words & Music by Ringo Starr.

I WANT YOU (She's so heavy)

Words & Music by John Lennon & Paul McCartney.

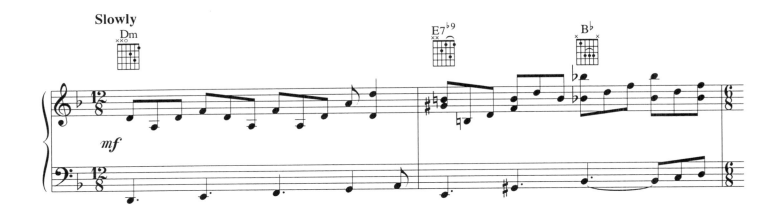

HERE COMES THE SUN

Words & Music by George Harrison.
© Copyright 1969 Harrisongs Limited.
All Rights Reserved. International Copyright Secured.

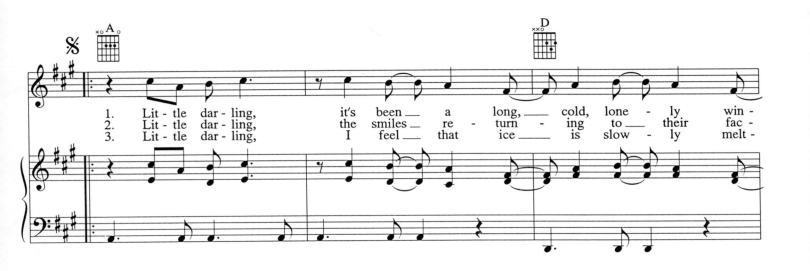

1. Lit - tle dar - ling, it's been ___ a long, ___ cold, lone - ly win -
2. Lit - tle dar - ling, the smiles re - turn - ing to ___ their fac -
3. Lit - tle dar - ling, I feel ___ that ice ___ is slow - ly melt -

- ter; Lit - tle dar - ling, it feels ___ like years ___ since it's ___ been here. ___
- es; Lit - tle dar - ling, it seems ___ like years ___ since it's ___ been here. ___
- ing; Lit - tle dar - ling, it seems ___ like years ___ since it's ___ been clear. ___

Here comes ___ the sun, ___   Here comes ___ the sun, ___

BECAUSE

Words & Music by John Lennon & Paul McCartney.
© Copyright 1969 Northern Songs, under licence to
MCA Music Limited, 77 Fulham Palace Road, London W6.
All Rights Reserved. International Copyright Secured.

cause the world is round, it turns me on; Be-
cause the wind is high, it blows my mind; Be-
cause the sky is blue, it makes me cry; Be-

cause _____ the world is round. Ah _____
cause _____ the wind is high.
cause _____ the sky is blue.

29

YOU NEVER GIVE ME YOUR MONEY

Words & Music by John Lennon & Paul McCartney.

step on the gas and wipe __ that tear a - way; __ One sweet dream __ came true.

To - day __ came true, __ to - day. __

Repeat and Fade

One, two, three, four, five, six, sev - en, All good chil - dren go to heav - en.

SUN KING

Words & Music by John Lennon & Paul McCartney.
© Copyright 1969 Northern Songs, under licence to
MCA Music Limited, 77 Fulham Palace Road, London W6.
All Rights Reserved. International Copyright Secured.

POLYTHENE PAM

Words & Music by John Lennon & Paul McCartney.
© Copyright 1969 Northern Songs, under licence to
CA Music Limited, 77 Fulham Palace Road, London W6.
All Rights Reserved. International Copyright Secured.

Bright 4

Well, you should

see Pol-y-thene Pam. She's so good look-ing, but she looks like a man.

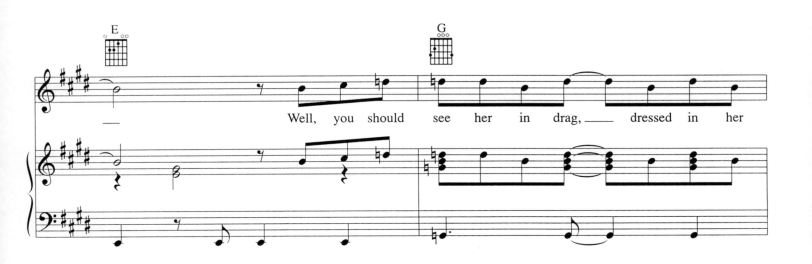

Well, you should see her in drag, ___ dressed in her

MEAN MR. MUSTARD

Words & Music by John Lennon & Paul McCartney.
© Copyright 1969 Northern Songs, under licence to
MCA Music Limited, 77 Fulham Palace Road, London W6.
All Rights Reserved. International Copyright Secured.

Moderately

1. Mean Mis-ter Mus-tard sleeps in the park, shaves in the dark, tryin' to save pa-per. __
2. His sis-ter Pam works in a shop, she nev-er stops, she's a go get-ter. __

__ Sleeps in a hole in the road, __
__ Takes him out to look at the Queen, __

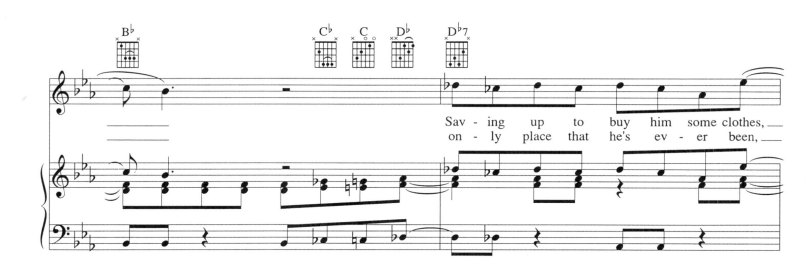

__ Sav-ing up to buy him some clothes, __
__ on-ly place that he's ev-er been, __

SHE CAME IN THROUGH THE BATHROOM WINDOW

Words & Music by John Lennon & Paul McCartney.
© Copyright 1969 Northern Songs, under licence to
MCA Music Limited, 77 Fulham Palace Road, London W6.
All Rights Reserved. International Copyright Secured.

GOLDEN SLUMBERS

Words & Music by John Lennon & Paul McCartney.

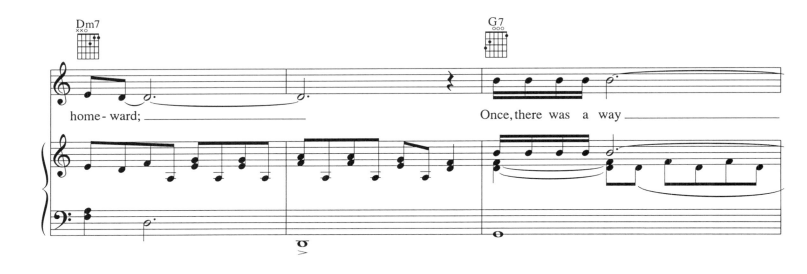

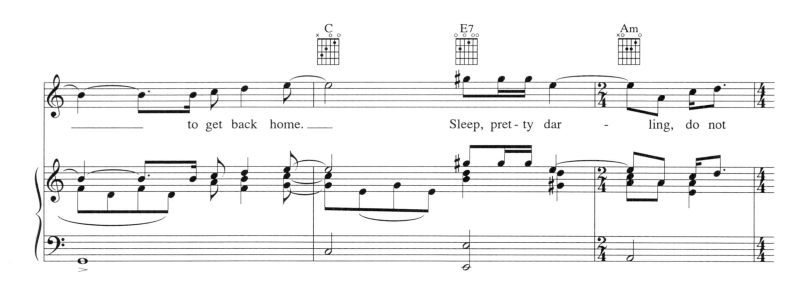

CARRY THAT WEIGHT

Words & Music by John Lennon & Paul McCartney.
© Copyright 1969 Northern Songs, under licence to
MCA Music Limited, 77 Fulham Palace Road, London W6.
All Rights Reserved. International Copyright Secured.

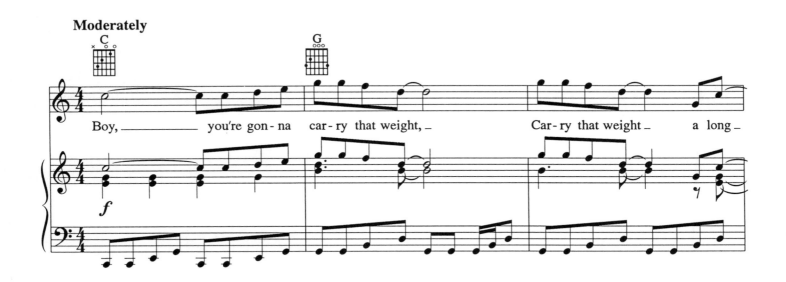

Boy, _____ you're gon-na car-ry that weight, _____ Car-ry that weight _____ a long _____

_____ time. Boy, _____ you're gon-na car-ry that weight, _____

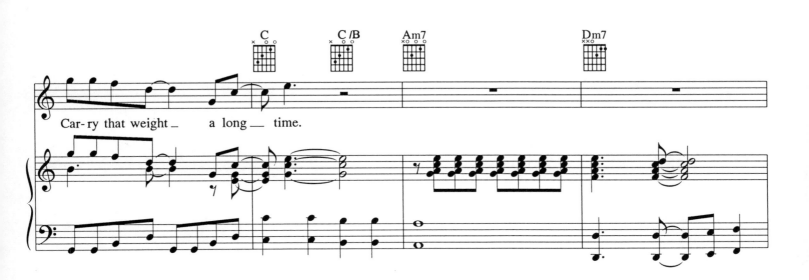

Car-ry that weight _____ a long _____ time.

I ne-ver give you my pil - low, ___ I on-ly send you my

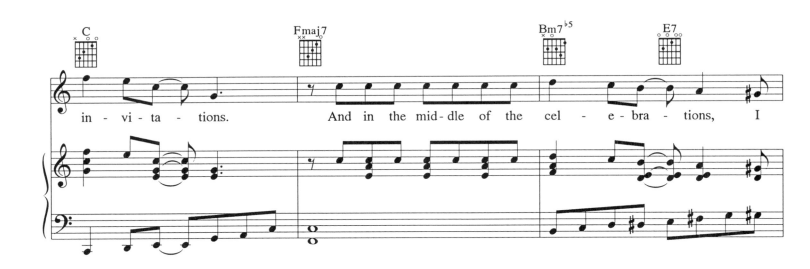

in - vi - ta - tions. And in the mid-dle of the cel - e - bra - tions, I

THE END

Words & Music by John Lennon & Paul McCartney.

Moderately fast

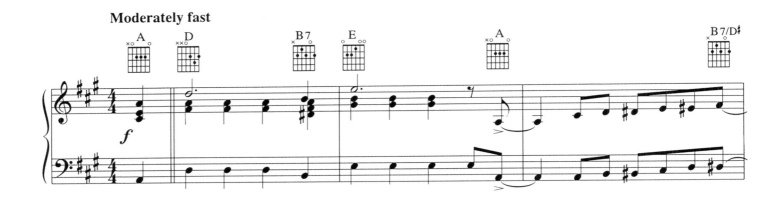

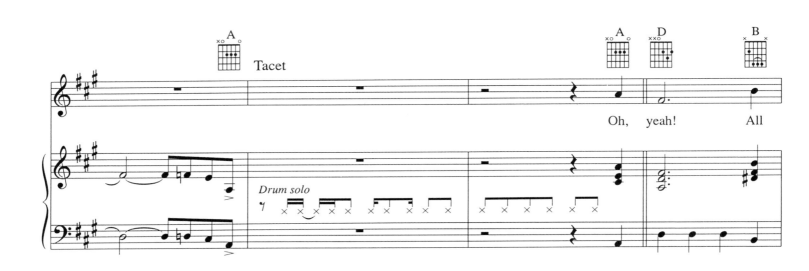

Oh, yeah! All

right! Are ____ you gon - na be in my dreams _____ to - night? _

Tacet

Drum solo

A7   D7   A7

D7   A7   D7

Love   you, ___   love   you, ___

love you, ___ love you, ___ Love you, ___

love you, ___ love you, ___ love you, ___

love you, ___ Love you, ___ love you, ___

love you, ___ love you, ___ love you, ___

HER MAJESTY

Words & Music by John Lennon & Paul McCartney.

Fairly Bright

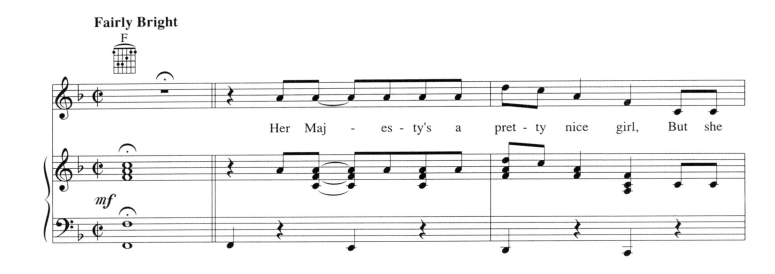

Her Maj - es - ty's a pret - ty nice girl, But she

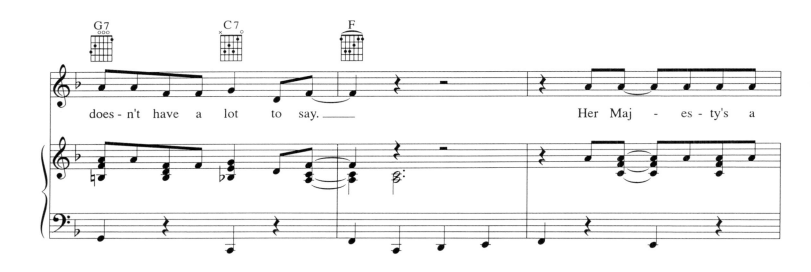

does - n't have a lot to say. ____ Her Maj - es - ty's a

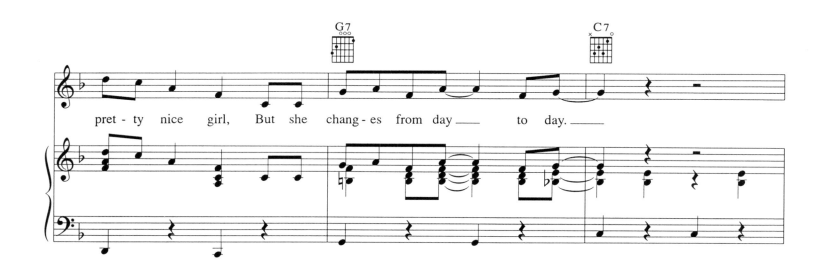

pret - ty nice girl, But she chang - es from day ____ to day. ____

The Beatles: Music Books In Print

The Best Of The Beatles: Book 1
NO18541

The Best Of The Beatles: Book 2
NO18558

The Best Of The Beatles: Book 3 Sgt. Pepper
NO18566

The Best Of The Beatles : Book 4
NO18608

The Best Of The Beatles: Book 5
NO18616

Beatles Big Note: Piano/Vocal Edition
NO17428

Beatles Big Note: Guitar Edition
NO17402

A Collection Of Beatles Oldies: Piano Vocal Edition
NO17659

A Collection Of Beatles Oldies: Guitar Edition
NO18004

The Beatles Complete: Piano/ Vocal/Easy Organ Edition
NO17162

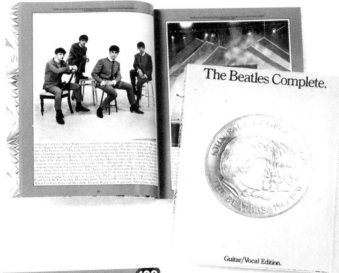

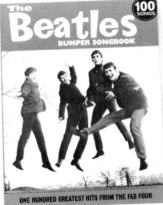

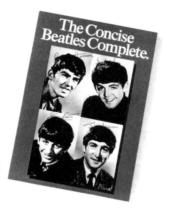

The Beatles Complete (Revised)
Re-engraved, revised edition of 'The Beatles Complete'. For piano/organ/ vocal, complete with lyrics and guitar chord symbols. Includes every song composed and recorded by the group. 203 songs, plus 24-page appreciation by Ray Connolly, lavishly illustrated with rare photographs.
Piano/Organ/Vocal Edition
NO18160
Guitar/Vocal Edition
NO18145

The Beatles Bumper Songbook
Full piano/vocal arrangements of 100 songs made famous by the Fab Four. Includes 'All You Need Is Love', 'Yellow Submarine', 'Lucy In The Sky With Diamonds' and 'Hey Jude', all complete with lyrics. 256 pages in all.
NO17998

The Concise Beatles Complete
NO18244

The Beatles Complete: Chord Organ Edition
NO17667

The Beatles Complete: Guitar Edition
NO17303

The Beatles: A Hard Day's Night
NO90542

Beatles For Sale
NO17584

The Beatles: Help
NO90541

The Beatles: Highlights
NO18525

The Beatles: Let It Be
NO90536

The Beatles: Love Songs
NO17915

The Beatles: Magical Mystery Tour
NO17600

The Beatles 1962-1966
NO17931

The Beatles 1967-70
NO17949

The Beatles: Revolver
NO90539

The Beatles Rock Score

Twelve numbers scored for groups. Perfect note-for-note transcriptions from the recordings for vocal and each instrument, in standard notation and guitar tablature. Includes drum line and lyrics.
NO18442

Rubber Soul
NO90540

The Singles Collection 1962-1970
NO90544

The 6 Chord Songbook
NO18418

The 6 Chord Songbook: Book 2
NO18517

20 Greatest Hits: Piano/Vocal Edition
NO18269

20 Greatest Hits: Easy Guitar
NO18277

White Album
NO90538

The Songs Of George Harrison
AM30990

The Great Songs Of George Harrison
AM37649

The Great Songs Of John Lennon
AM61854

101 Beatles Songs For Buskers
Includes all their favourite songs in melody line arrangements, complete with lyrics and guitar chord boxes.
Piano/Organ Edition.
NO18392

Beatles Best for Keyboard
HD10029

The Complete Keyboard Player: The Beatles
NO18509

The Complete Piano Player Beatles
NO18806

Creative Keyboard Series: The Beatles
AM71911

Home Organist Library: Volume 9 Beatles Songs
NO18186

The Beatles. 100 Hits For All Keyboards
Special lay-flat, spiral-bound collection of favourite Beatles songs arranged for all keyboards – piano, electronic piano, organ and portable keyboards. With full lyrics.
NO18590

It's Easy To Play Beatles
NO17907

It's Easy To Play Beatles 2
NO90342

SFX-3: Beatles Hits
AM33093

SFX-16: Beatles Hits 2
AM39660

Beatles Guitar: Tablature
NO18798

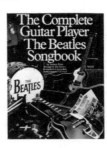

The Complete Guitar Player: The Beatles
NO18491

The Beatles For Classical Guitar
NO17444

The Beatles For Classical Guitar: Book 2
NO17782

Fingerpicking Beatles
AM30941

Beatles For Recorder
NO18434

Greatest Hits For Harmonica
NO18673

Beatles: Themes And Variations: Clarinet
NO17873

Beatles: Themes And Variations: Flute
NO17865

Beatles: Themes And Variations: Trumpet
NO17881

Lennon & McCartney For Clarinet
NO17725

Lennon & McCartney For Clarinet
NO18764

Lennon & McCartney For Flute
NO18756

Lennon & McCartney For Saxophone
NO18772

Lennon & McCartney For Trumpet
NO17733

Lennon & McCartney For Trumpet
NO18780

Lennon & McCartney 60 Greatest For Trumpet
NO18715

Beatles Für Die Blockflöte
MG13582

Die Beatles Für Klassische Gitarre: Band 1
MG13202

The Beatles Apart
PRP10083

The Beatles Book
OP43439

The Complete Beatles Lyrics
OP42027

With The Beatles: The Historic Photographs Of Dezo Hoffmann
OP41961

Beatles: In Their Own Words
OP40419

Paul McCartney: In His Own Words
OP40047

Available from all good Music Shops.

In case of difficulty, please contact:
Music Sales Limited
Newmarket Road, Bury St. Edmunds, Suffolk IP33 3YB, England.
Telephone: 0284 702600. Fax: 0284 768301. Telex: 817845.

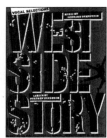